DR. RODERICK VAN DANIEL

TITLE

IX

Gender Discrimination

TITLE
IX

◆

Roderick Van Daniel, Ph. D. & J.D.

Van Daniel Marketing, LLC
Aberdeen Birmingham Memphis Atlanta

TITLE IX

Van Daniel Marketing, LLC

For information address:
Van Daniel Marketing, LLC
vandanielmarketing@hotmail.com
www.vandanielmarketing.webs.com

Printed in the United States of America

"Women are supposed to be calm; but women feel just as men feel."

   - Charlotte Bronte

"Success is not about how much money you make, it is about the difference you make in people's lives."

   - Michelle Obama

"You have to accept whatever comes and the only important thing is that you meet it with courage and with the best that you have to give."

   - Eleanor Roosevelt

Contents

◆

For my mother,
Yvonne Daniel

Acknowledgement

◆

This book is dedicated to my mother, Yvonne Daniel, for listening to my dreams, encouraging me to achieve my goals, and providing the support for me to be strong. Mom, you have inspired me from the moment you gave birth to me. I love you. You instilled in me the importance of education but more importantly to graduate with the degree. Thanks for always encouraging me to keep the Lord with me on my educational journey and in my everyday life. Mom, thank you for the financial support. I never would have made it without you. I love you so much.

This book is also dedicated to my brothers, Dashmond and Zerdock, sister, Ashalond Daniel, and my father Roy Garth. You gave me strength each day. Thank you for believing that dreams do come true; I did it!

To my grandmother, Clara Betts Daniel, thank you for instilling the Lord in my life. I miss you. Thank you for telling me that I have to be strong to survive in this world.

Thank you for telling me to hold my head up high and not walk with it down. Thank you for making me come inside the house before the street lights came on at night. I want to thank you for loving me and telling me that you have to leave the nest sometimes to truly become the man that you desire to become. Thank you for telling me to carry the Lord's scripture in my pocket every day, "The Lord is my shepard; I shall not want." I thank you for being strong; you made me strong through being around you. You lived to be in your nineties; you gave me wisdom and strength beyond my childhood years. I miss you. I love you still. Only the strong survive, you told me to remember that always. I stand strong for you and my family. I thank you.

To Dr. Prince, Judge Aycock, and Coach Ball-Williamson; I also thank you for giving me an opportunity to learn from your wisdom. I value you all.

Thank you God and Jesus for I can do all things because you all strengthen me. Thanks for making me strong in your word and truth; I love you both as well.

Life Situations

Life Situations

Today is your day......

Every day, we live in this life trying to be better today than we were yesterday. We must treat each other fairly in this world. But sometimes as humans, we are faced with discrimination in some form or another. Today, tell yourself to stand up and believe in your future. I grew up in the South within the United States of America; Mississippi to be exact. Aberdeen, Mississippi to be even more direct to the point and location of my journey and struggles of living in rural America and also facing the challenges of adjusting to life in urban America. I live in Birmingham, Alabama.

I hoped to be writing one day to transform the minds of the individuals; the people that have familiar backgrounds as me. Living in different urban cities in America has built my mind to

understand the difference between urban and rural America;
societal problems exist in both communities.

We must push forward through the unfairness of hatred and
move in your heart to a place of peace. Find your inner peace
through not allowing hurtful tactics of others to dictate your
future. Live life to the best of your ability and never give up
on your life getting better each day.

Be amazing......

Open your mind to know that discrimination is alive and well.
Believe that you can be the change that will move our nation and
world forward. Today, we will talk about gender discrimination.
Remember to love and not hate. We all are amazing people in the
inner most places in our hearts.

"Life Situations"

The Law

The Law

Gender discrimination is unfairness towards women in the work environment, education, sports, and in life. Women usually are excluded in opportunities especially in the past that men tend to be given a fair chance to succeed. Sexual harassment, participation in education and sports, equal pay are major issues that women face day to day in our country and the world.

Sexual harassment is a violation on a woman constitutional right under the Civil Rights Act of 1964. Sexual harassment is any unwanted sexual advance, request for sexual favors, and any other verbal or physical conduct of sexual nature. Some people may say that words are only words and a friendly touch of the opposite sex is okay. However, you can say words or touch someone and not intend anything, but it is the perception of the person to whom the act was made that determines if it is harassment.

Title IX was enacted by Congress in 1972 to prohibit gender discrimination in the nation education program. This also includes the arena of sports. Title IX has changed the participation for women in the work environment drastically since the 1970s but in a beneficial and positive form.

Title IX states:

"No person in the United States shall, on the basis of sex, be excluded from participation in, be denied the benefits of, or be subjected to discrimination under any education program or activity receiving any educational program or activity receiving Federal financial assistance."

Most institutions satisfy the requirement of Title IX through the benchmark: "participation opportunities for male and female students are provided in numbers that are 'substantially proportional' to their respective enrollment. Title IX is continuing to help women progress in 2016. I hope more women will continue to get their opportunities to make their dreams reality in their chosen field of endeavor and also receive "equal pay" for the great work they do along the way.

Equal pay was a major issue in the past and also presently. I think progress has been made in all arenas for women since Title IX and the Civil Rights Act have been mandated. So, women stay positive on your journey and continue to dream your dreams. Make them your reality. The law is on your side.

"The Law"

The Future

The Future

Equal protection is big from the constitutional perspective. Equal protection requires that no person be singled out from similarly situated people, or different benefits bestowed or burdens imposed, under a constitutional permissible reason exists for doing so. So, the future is bright for the women of our century. Continue to be strong and amazing as you are today and every day of your life.

Keep moving forward......

A lot of doors are opening up for you; so take advantage of the opportunities. Never let anyone tell you that you cannot be a success. You all have made a significant impact on our country and the world.

Never give up on your dreams......

Eleanor Roosevelt stated, "With a new day, comes strength and new thoughts."

The future is your next second of your life that you breathe air within your lungs in life; so make positive steps to making your day amazing. Do not let the injustices and discrimination hinder you from being the best you that you can be in 2016 and so on.

Michelle Obama stated, "Success is not about how much money you make, it is about the difference you make in people's lives."

"The Future"

Express Your Thoughts

Express Your Thoughts

"You can triumph and come to skill. You can be great if you only will. You are well equipped for what fight you choose. You have legs and arms and a brain to use. And the man who has risen great deeds to do; began his life with no more than YOU."

 - Edgar A. Guest

Express Your Thoughts

"How important it is for us to recognize and celebrate our heroes
and she - roes"

- Maya Angelo

Express Your Thoughts

_____

_____

_____

_____

_____

_____

_____

_____

_____

_____

"Ladies will not hold ourselves bound by any Laws in which we have no voice, or Representation."

‒ Abigail Adams

Express Your Thoughts

"Forgiveness is a way of opening up the doors again and moving forward,
whether in a personal life or a national life."

- Hillary Clinton

Express Your Thoughts

_____

_____

_____

_____

_____

_____

_____

_____

"The climb is different even though the destination is the same. Ultimately, it all depends on 'What I want' which determines success."

 - Anuranjita Kuma

Express Your Thoughts

"I would like to be remembered as a person who wanted to be free, so other people would be also free."

- Rosa Parks

Express Your Thoughts

"Surround yourself with people who are going to lift you higher."

- Oprah Winfrey

Express Your Thoughts

"This I recall to my mind, therefore have I hope. It is of the Lord's mercies that we are not consumed, because his compassions fail not. They are new every morning: great is thy faithfulness. The Lord is my portion, saith my soul; therefore will I hope in him. The Lord is good unto them that wait for him, to the soul that seeketh him. It is good that a man should both hope and quietly wait for the salvation of the Lord."

Lamentations 3:21-26

Express Your Thoughts

"When we do the best we can, we never know what miracle is wrought in our life, or in the life of another."

– Helen Keller

Express Your Thoughts

_____

_____

_____

_____

_____

_____

_____

_____

_____

"Keep your mind focus on your goals. Do not let the distractions of life hold you back from accomplishing your tasks in life. Live long and strong. Success."

   - Dr. Roderick Van Daniel

Express Your Thoughts

"Never stop giving your best even when the world tells you that your best is not good enough. Success."

- Dr. Roderick Van Daniel

Express Your Thoughts

"Do not mistake politeness for lack of strength."

-   Sonya Sotomayor

Express Your Thoughts

"Believe in your aspirations in life. Believe in yourself. Have a strategy. Make it become your reality. Success."

- Dr. Roderick Van Daniel

Express Your Thoughts

"Those who hope in the Lord will renew their strength. They will soar on wings like eagles; they will run and not grow weary, they will walk and not be faint."

   - Isaiah 40:31

Express Your Thoughts

"But hope that is seen is no hope at all. Who hopes for what he already have, we wait for it patiently. In the same way, the Spirit helps us in our weakness. We do not know what we ought to pray for, but the Spirit himself intercedes for us with groans that words cannot express. And he who searches our hearts knows the mind of the Spirit."

    - Romans 8:24-27

Express Your Thoughts

"Now faith is being sure of what we hope for and certain of what we do not see. And without faith it is impossible to please God, because anyone who comes to him must believe that he exists and that he rewards those who earnestly seek him."

— Hebrews 11:1,6

Conclusion

Conclusion

Hold on to your strength from within; you are an amazing person. Do not let anyone tell you differently. Do not let discrimination hinder your process towards personal growth.

Maya Angelo stated, "Life is not measured by the number of breaths we take, but by the moments that take our breath away."

Dr. Roderick Van Daniel

Dr. Roderick Van Daniel is an author. He presently lives in Birmingham, Alabama. I believe life is deep and unresolved from a lot of untruths and truths. We are all amazing people.

Contact: roddaniel205@gmail.com

www.ingramcontent.com/pod-product-compliance
Lightning Source LLC
Chambersburg PA
CBHW020948180526
45163CB00006B/2367

ISBN 9781523887866

Darío de Regoyos
Émile Verhaeren

España negra